Made in the USA
Columbia, SC
16 November 2020

24734578R00043

More Great Bass Books from Fundamental Changes

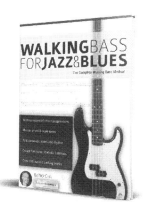

Walking Bass for Jazz and Blues

- Discover a Complete Method to Learn Jazz and Blues Walking Bass
- Master Arpeggios and Concepts to play like the Masters
- Develop a full range of Scales, Arpeggios and Soloing to create your own Walking Bass Lines

The Bass Technique Finger Gym

- Proven technical exercises to supercharge your progress
- Turn technique into licks with essential lick-building exercises
- Learn to build speed, slap and pop

Chord Tone Soloing for Bass Guitar

- Master Jazz Arpeggios and use them like a pro in your solos
- Learn how to solo over 13 Essential Progressions
- Spice up your bass skills with Extensions and Substitutions

Sight Reading Mastery for Bass Guitar

- Pitch Recognition
- Instant Location of Notes
- Unlimited Exercises
- All Keys

WALKING BASS
FOR JAZZ&BLUES

The Complete Walking Bass Method

NICK CLARK

FUNDAMENTAL CHANGES

Walking Bass for Jazz & Blues

The Complete Walking Bass Method

By Nick Clark

Published by **www.fundamental-changes.com**

ISBN: 978-1-911267-96-6

www.fundamental-changes.com

Twitter: @guitar_joseph

Over 10,000 fans on Facebook: **FundamentalChangesInGuitar**

Instagram: **FundamentalChanges**

For over 350 Free Guitar Lessons with Videos Check Out

www.fundamental-changes.com

Cover Image Copyright: Shutterstock

Contents

Introduction

What exactly is a walking bassline? A walking bassline generally consists of notes of equal duration and intensity (typically 1/4 notes) that create a feeling of forward motion. It is possible to add in rhythmic skips and pauses, but in general, a walking bassline drives the song forward, step by step.

So how do you walk? Start by putting one note in front of the other!

In this book, you will find practical, concise instruction for building musical walking basslines. This book sorts through the wealth of information available and boils it down to the most practical and important aspects of playing walking bass.

The purpose of a good walking bassline (or any bassline for that matter) is twofold: First, to outline the current chord being played, and second to smoothly approach the next chord. The main point to consider when constructing walking basslines is how to create a smooth transition between the last note of the current chord and the first note of the next. In general, we make this transition smooth by limiting the interval between these two notes to either a half step (semitone), whole step (tone) or a perfect 5th. The essence of a walking bassline is created by playing *four to the bar*, which means we play four 1/4 notes per measure.

First, we will take an in-depth look at building basslines using roots, 5ths and arpeggios. From there, we will add chromatic and scalar tones, and then boil it all down to some practical patterns that can be used over any chord change. Along the way, we'll apply these basslines to common jazz and blues chord progressions.

While the examples are based on jazz and blues music, this book provides the tools necessary to develop your own walking lines in other styles of music, such as blues, country, rockabilly, rock 'n' roll and many others. This book also discusses some of the theory behind the concepts in each chapter. However, if the theory is all new to you, I recommend reading **Modern Music Theory for Guitarists** by Joseph Alexander.

So, with that, grab your bass, cue the audio examples and let's make some music!

Get the Audio

The audio files for this book are available to download for free from www.fundamental-changes.com. The link is in the top right-hand corner. Simply select this book title from the drop-down menu and follow the instructions to get the audio.

We recommend that you download the files directly to your computer, not to your tablet, and extract them there before adding them to your media library. You can then put them on your tablet, iPod or burn them to CD. On the download page there is a help PDF and we also provide technical support via the contact form.

For over 350 Free Lessons with Videos Check out:

www.fundamental-changes.com

Over 10,000 fans on Facebook: **FundamentalChangesInGuitar**

Instagram: **FundamentalChanges**

Chapter One - Building Basslines with Arpeggios

The most common chord movement in both blues and jazz (not to mention rock, pop and country) follows the *Circle of 5ths*, where chords descend in intervals of perfect 5ths – for example from D to G to C. This can also be thought of as ascending in intervals of perfect 4ths[1].

We'll refer to this movement in Roman numerals as I to IV. Since this movement makes up the majority of the chord changes we encounter in jazz, we will begin by looking at walking basslines that outline this movement.

Moving from I to IV

The root is the most important note for a bass player to play on the first beat of each chord. Since a chord's harmony is heard from the bottom up, it is important to define the chord by emphasizing the root note in the bass. There are times when other notes can be used, but for now we will concentrate on the root.

We will begin by playing whole notes over each chord.

Example 1a:

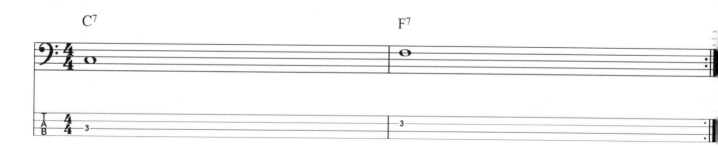

These notes form the foundation of the chords, but since they don't provide any forward movement, it's not a walking bassline. There are times when this could be just what the song needs, but for now we will use it as a foundation and move on.

The next most common note to add is the 5th of the chord. Many great basslines are built using little more than the root and the 5th. The neck diagram below shows the location of the 5th in relation to the root. Memorize this pattern because it forms the most important interval a bass player can have under their fingers.

---

1. Moving *down five notes* from G to C, G – F – E – D, is the same as moving *up four notes* from G to C, G – A – B – C.

Roots and 5ths

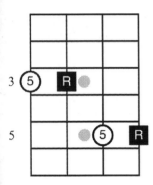

Let's incorporate the 5th of the chord into our bassline by playing half notes with the root on beat one and the 5th on beat three.

Example 1b:

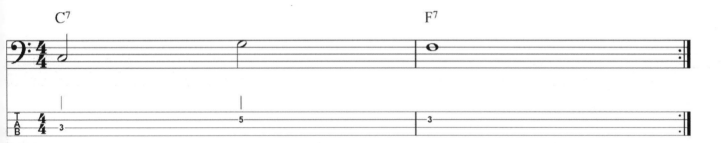

Next, we will play four 1/4 notes per bar to develop the familiar walking bassline feel. We were not concerned with chord quality (Major or Minor) when playing only roots and 5ths, but we now need to expand our note choice to better outline the chords.

We'll begin with the four-note C7 arpeggio. This is a *Dominant* seventh chord and consists of the root (C), Major 3rd (E), perfect 5th (G) and Minor 7th (Bb). The neck diagram below shows the notes of the C7 arpeggio on the neck.

The short formula for a Dominant 7 arpeggio is 1 3 5 b7.

'7' Arpeggio

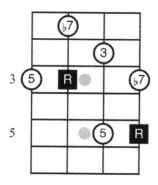

The order of arpeggio notes we play is shown in the brackets for each example.

Example 1c shows the arpeggio notes in ascending order.

Example 1c: [1-3-5-b7]

Playing the ascending arpeggio outlines the chord nicely and sounds great over some chord progressions. However, it doesn't approach the root (F) of the F7 chord very smoothly.

In Example 1d, we mix up the order of the arpeggio notes to create a smooth, whole step transition from the 5th of the C7 chord (G) down to the root of the F7 chord.

Example 1d: [1-b7-3-5]

In Example 1e, we will approach the F7 chord from below. This time we are approaching from a half step by playing the 3rd of the C7 chord (E).

Example 1e: [1-b7-5-3]

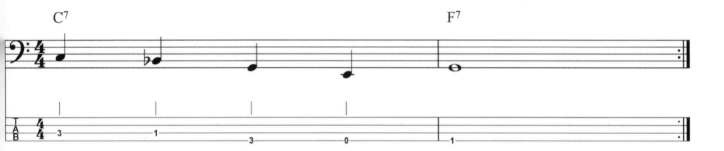

It is not necessary to play every note in the arpeggio. The previous examples rearranged the four notes of the C7 arpeggio to approach the root of the F7 chord by whole and half steps from above and below, respectively. Consider the possibilities of leaving out one or two chord tones and repeating others.

Examples 1f though 1i show several patterns of chord tones which approach from below, while examples 1j and 1m approach from above. Note the repetition of the root on beats one and two in some patterns, while the octave is played in others. There are many more combinations than I have shown here, so feel free to experiment with some of your own.

Example 1f: [1-1-3-5]

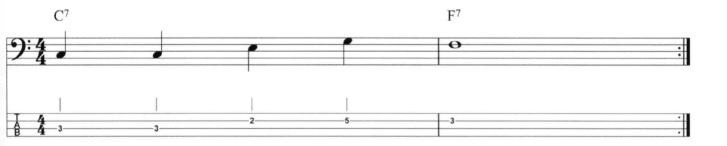

Example 1g: [1-5-8-5]

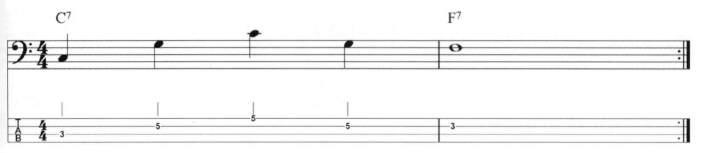

Example 1h: [8-5-3-5]

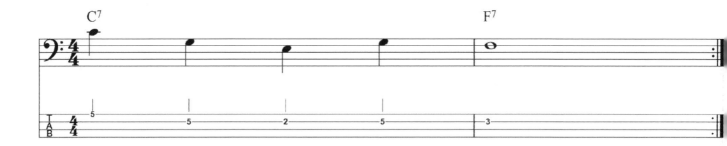

Example 1i: [1-8-7-5]

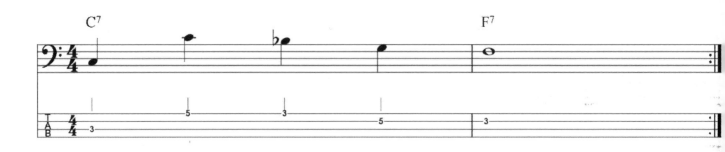

Example 1j: [1-1-5-3]

Example 1k: [1-3-5-3]

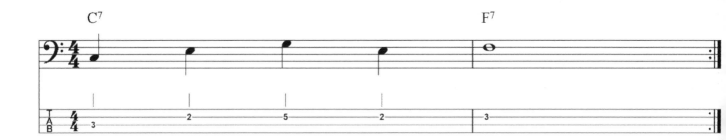

Example 1l: [8-b7-5-3]

Example 1m: [1-5-8-3]

So far, we have approached the root of the F7 chord by whole-steps-from-above and half-steps-from-below. Next we'll learn to approach the root by an interval of a perfect 5th. This means the approach note on beat four of the C7 chord will be a perfect 5th away from the *target* chord note of F.

The note a perfect 5th away from the F is C (which is also the root of the C7 chord). The strongest chord movement in blues and jazz is a descending 5th, so we are applying the same idea to the notes of our bassline.

Examples 1n though 1q depict several patterns that approach the root of the F7 chord by a perfect 5th (C note).

Example 1n: [1-1-5-1]

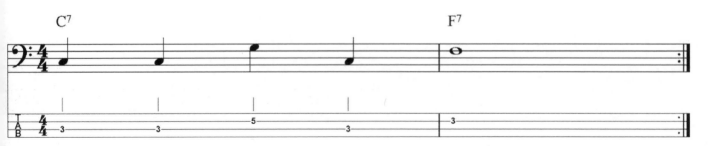

Example 1o: [1-3-5-1]

Example 1p: [8-3-5-1]

Example 1q: [8-b7-5-1]

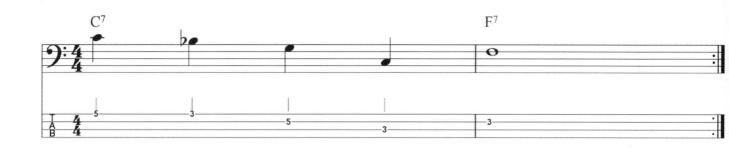

Table 1a: Summary of Bassline Patterns

Approach from Above	[1-b7-3-5] [1-1-3-5] [1-5-8-5] [8-5-3-5] [1-8-b7-5]
Approach from Below	[1-b7-5-3] [1-1-5-3] [1-3-5-3] [8-b7-5-3] [1-5-8-3]
Approach from a 5th	[1-1-5-1] [1-3-5-1] [8-3-5-1] [8-b7-5-1]

Think of these chord tones as the skeleton of the bassline. By playing only the arpeggios, the bassline sounds a little boney, and we may wish to add other notes to flesh it out.

When adding other notes, we need to eliminate some of the chord tones and, with careful consideration, we can outline the chord sufficiently with a chord tone or two, and use other scale notes to add interest and melody.

Chapter Two – Basslines with Chromatic and Scale Tones

The previous chapter discussed building skeletal basslines using roots, 5ths and arpeggio tones. In this chapter, we'll begin to fill out those lines using chromatic and scalar notes.

In Example 1d, we used only chord tones, and transitioned a whole step from the G of the C7 chord to the F of the F7 chord.

Example 1d: [1-b7-3-5]

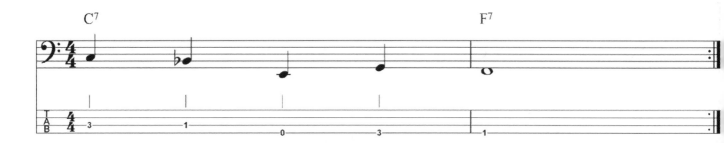

We can smooth the transition further by changing the whole step to a half step (chromatic).

Example 2a: [1-b7-5-b5]

Another option is to replace the b7th on beat two with the Major 3rd (E).

Example 2b: [1-3-5-b5]

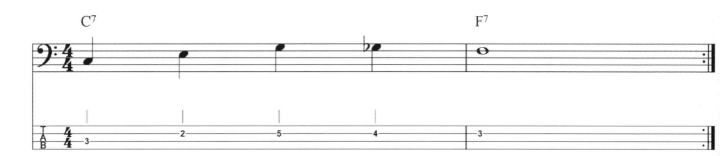

Let's take the same idea and approach the root of the F7 chord from a half step below. In Example 1e, we approached the F from below. However, since the Major 3rd of the C7 is an E and played on beat four, we were already approaching the F root from a half step.

Example 1e: [1-b7-5-3]

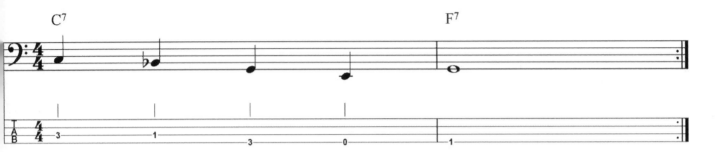

In this case, we can add a chromatic note *before* the E note, which sets up two half steps into the F7 root.

Example 2c: [1-b7-b3-3]

In Example 2d, we approach the F7 from below in the same way, except we move from the root to the 5th of the C7 chord on beat two.

Example 2d: [1-5-b3-3]

Until now, we have mainly focused on playing chord tones on beats one, two and three, and a chromatic approach note on beat four. Now, let's use other notes from the scale. Using the 2nd, 4th and 6th can smooth out the basslines while continuing to outline each chord in the sequence.

One essential pattern to have in your arsenal is shown in Example 2e. Known as the "chromatic walk up", it can be applied to any chord change. You play the root of the C7 chord, and then approach the root of the F7 chord with three consecutive half steps (semitones).

You have probably heard this pattern used in many different styles, not just in jazz and blues. To hear it in classic rock, listen to the bass and guitar line in the outro of "Hey Joe" by Jimi Hendrix.

Example 2e: [1-2-b3-3]

Example 2f doesn't include a 3rd, which gives it a more neutral sound. This pattern is, however, extremely easy to visualize and play and it works well over both Major and Minor chords.

Example 2f: [1-2-5-b5]

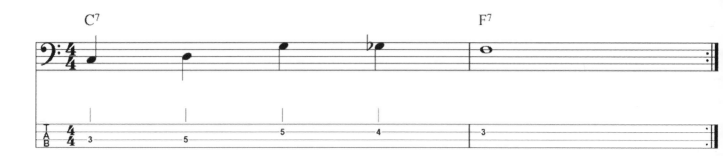

During the bop era of jazz in 1940s and 1950s, many soloists played in a style known as "change running", where they outlined the quickly moving chord changes much as a bassist would do. One of the most common patterns is shown in Example 2g.

Example 2g: [1-2-3-5]

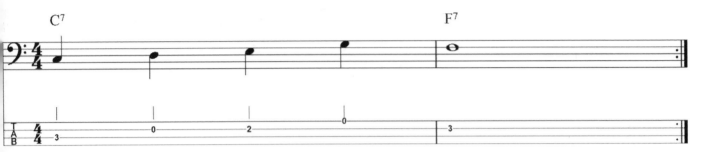

Example 2h is similar to the previous example, but the Major 3rd (E) is replaced by the Major 6th (A) on beat three. The Major 6th has a melodic sound similar to the Major 3rd and blends well with the other chord tones.

Example 2h: [1-2-6-5]

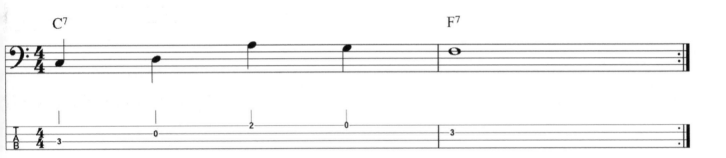

In Example 2i, we replace the Major 2nd (D) with the Major 3rd (E), which gives it an arpeggio like sound.

Example 2i: [1-3-6-5]

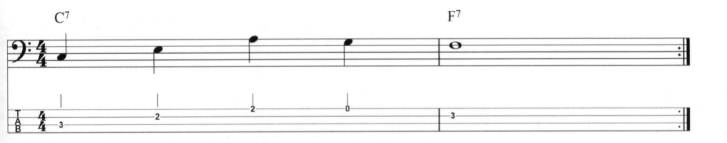

In Example 2j we walk down the scale until we hit the root of the F7 chord, approaching it from a whole step above.

17

Example: 2j [1-b7-6-5]

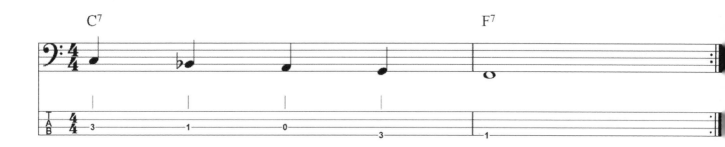

In Example 2k, we play the root twice and walk up the scale.

Example 2k: [1-1-2-3]

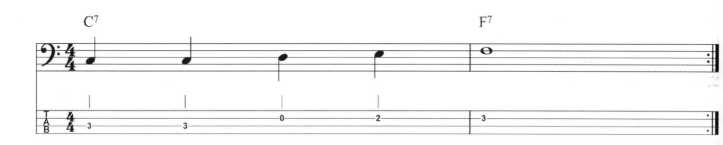

Table 2a summarizes the patterns developed in this chapter. We have developed many patterns for moving from I to IV, but you only need to know a few to create an interesting bassline!

Table 2a: Summary of Bassline Patterns

Approach from Above	[1-b7-5-b5] [1-3-5-b5] [1-2-5-b5] [1-2-3-5]
	[1-2-6-5] [1-3-6-5] [1-b7-6-5]
Approach from Below	[1-b7-b3-3] [1-5-b3-3] [1-2-b3-3] [1-1-2-3]

So far, we have taken an analytical approach to creating walking basslines by placing specific chord tones on specific beats and approaching the chord change in specific ways. This is to help you understand how these lines are created, get the sound in your head and the feel under your fingers, so you can decide which patterns you like.

The next step is to use them to create your own lines! Soon they will become part of your muscle and aural memory, and you won't even have to think of the intervals for each bar you play.

Chapter Three – The Blues Chord Progression

We have analysed and created walking bassline patterns for chords moving from I to IV. While this is the most common chord movement in blues and jazz, it is not the only one. Throughout the rest of the book, we will look at many other common chord movements you will encounter in blues and jazz.

It is important to develop bassline patterns for the traditional Twelve-Bar Blues chord progression. The blues is used in everything from rock to country to jazz, and this progression lays down the framework for many blues and jazz standards, as well as early rock 'n' roll classics. While there are many variations on the Twelve-Bar Blues, the following version is the most common.

Twelve-Bar Blues

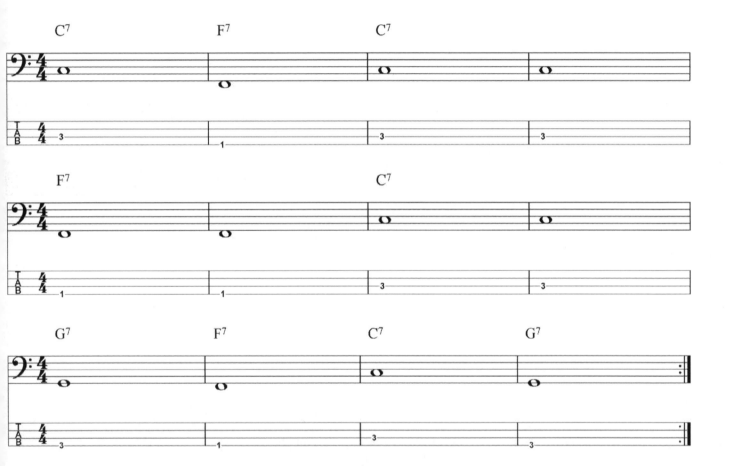

Static Chords

One of the most common chord progressions to learn is not a progression at all, but instead multiple bars of the same chord. Sometimes playing over one chord can be more challenging than playing over changing chords. When chords change, you are forced to select different notes. When staying on one chord, you have to get more creative to keep the music interesting.

The most common place to see multiple bars of the same chord is in the first four bars of the Twelve-Bar Blues. Since we are playing multiple bars of the same chord, we don't have to restrict our patterns to one bar only.

One of the most common two-bar patterns is the boogie pattern, shown in Example 3a. If you don't already know this one, it's time to get it under your fingers. Entire basslines have consisted of this pattern alone!

Example 3a: [1-3-5-6-b7-6-5-3]

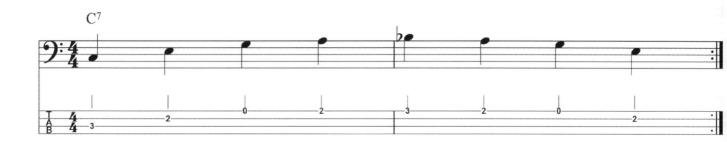

Example 3b is a variation on this pattern and has more of a rockabilly feel to it (Brian Setzer uses this pattern a lot in his rhythm playing). Both patterns also sound great when slapped on an upright bass!

Example 3b [1-3-4-b5-5-4-3-2]

In both these patterns, notice that the root is *not* played on the first beat of bar two, but instead another chord tone is played. In Example 3a it was the b7th (Bb) and in Example 3b it was the 5th (G). Since we have established the tonality of the C7 chord in the first bar, we can choose another chord tone for beat one of the second bar. We will explore this concept more in Chapter Nine.

The patterns in Example 3c consist of only one bar each, so they can be repeated for multiple bars of the same chord or used in combination with other patterns. Entire basslines have also been written with the 1-5-b7-7 pattern. Just listen to the bassline in "Oh Yeah" by Johnny A.

Example 3c: [1-3-1-5] [1-5-1-3] [1-b7-6-b7] [1-5-b7-7]

Moving from chord I to V

Chords moving up a perfect 5th (I to V) are also extremely common in blues and jazz. Along with the static chords (and I to IV movement), these changes make up most of the blues progression.

Example 3d approaches the G7 chromatically from below. This is the same pattern used in the first bar of the static chord Example 3b.

Example 3d: [1-3-4-b5]

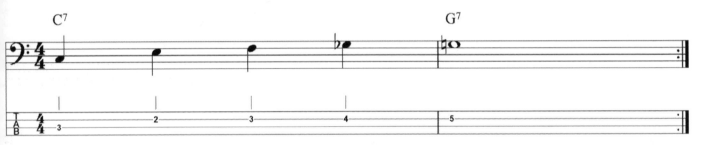

Examples 3e and 3f both approach the root of the G7 chord chromatically from above. Example 3e is a standard descent into the chord change, whereas Example 3f is more melodic thanks to the Major 3rd (E) and Major 6th (A).

Example 3e: [1-b7-6-b6]

Example 3f: [1-3-6-b6]

Example 3g walks up the scale, approaching the root of the G7 chord from a whole step below.

Example 3g: [1-2-3-4]

Example 3h approaches the root of the G7 chord from a D note, which is the interval of a perfect 5th away.

Example 3h: [1-b7-6-2]

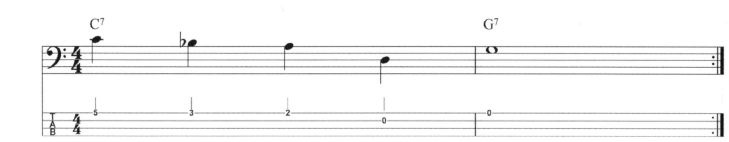

Moving from V to IV

This movement can also be thought of as descending a whole step. It is an integral part of playing the blues, where the V chord descends to the IV chord in bars nine and ten.

Examples 3i and 3j use only chord tones to descend chromatically to the root of the F7 chord.

Example 3i: [1-5-1-b7]

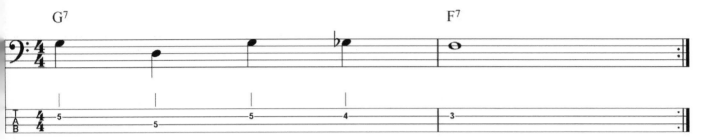

Example 3j: [1-3-1-b7]

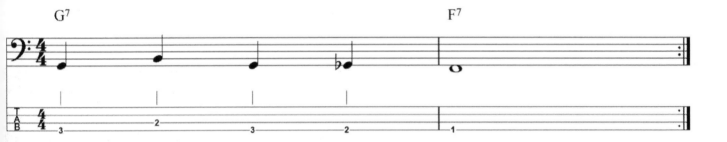

Example 3k is the first half of the boogie pattern that we developed in Example 3a, this time over a G7 chord. That pattern took us up to the b7th and back down to the root, but in this case the b7th (F) is as far as we need to go.

Example 3k: [1-3-5-6]

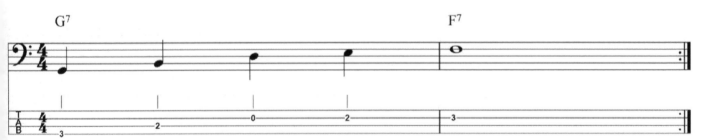

Example 3l is a Major triad arpeggio that approaches the root of F7 chord from above.

Example 3l: [1-3-5-8]

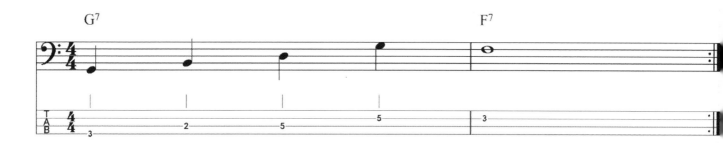

Example 3m walks up the scale to the C, which approaches the root of the F7 chord by a perfect 5th from below.

Example 3m: [1-2-3-4]

Example 3n is a root-5th-octave pattern that drops to the 6th (E) to approach the root of the F7 chord by a half step from below.

Example 3n: [1-5-8-6]

Table 3a: Summary of Bassline Patterns

Static Chord	[1-3-5-6-b7-6-5-3] [1-3-4-b5-5-4-3-2]
	[1-3-1-5] [1-5-1-3] [1-b7-6-b7] [1-5-b7-7]
I to V	[1-2-3-4] [1-3-4-b5] [1-b7-6-b6]
	[1-3-6-b6] [8-b7-6-2]
V to IV	[1-2-3-4] [1-5-1-b7] [1-3-1-b7]
	[1-3-5-6] [1-3-5-8] [1-5-8-6]

Now that we have developed patterns for all the chord changes we see in the blues, let's play through a full example. Example 3o contains a complete Twelve-Bar Blues bassline using just a few of the patterns we have developed so far. The patterns are not shown, so it's up to you to identify which patterns are being played. Play through this as written first, then substitute a few of the other patterns that you like the sound of.

Example 3o: Twelve-Bar Blues:

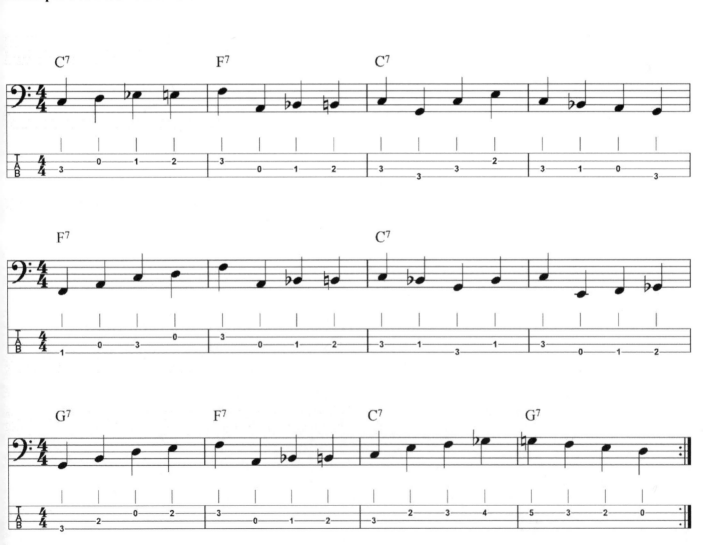

Chapter Four – The Major ii-V-I

Along with the blues, another common chord progression in jazz is the Major ii-V-I (two-five-one). This pattern consists of the seventh chords constructed from the 1st (I), 2nd (ii) and 5th (V) degrees of the Major scale.

When we harmonize the Major scale, the chord built of the root is a Major seventh (Maj7)(1-3-5-7), the chord built off the 2nd is a Minor seventh (m7)(1-b3-5-b7) and the chord built off the 5th is a Dominant seventh chord (7)(1-3-5-b7).

Example 4a shows a ii-V-I in the key of C, outlined with roots and 5ths. In this progression, Dm7 to G7 is the ii to V movement, and G7 to Cmaj7 is the V to I movement.

Notice, however, that these chords also descend by a perfect 5th/ascend by a perfect 4th, just like the I to IV movement we have studied so far. Therefore, we can apply the patterns we developed for the I to IV movement to our ii to V, and V to I movements.

Chord ii is Dm7

Chord V is G7

Chord I is CMaj7

Example 4a:

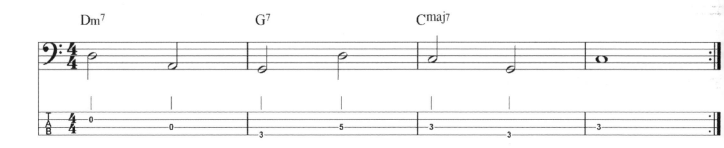

In Chapter One, we introduced the pattern for the Dominant 7 (7) arpeggio on the neck. The neck diagrams below show the patterns for the Minor 7th (m7) and Major 7th (Maj7) arpeggios, respectively.

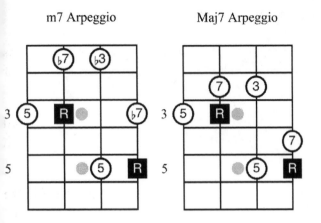

m7 Arpeggio   Maj7 Arpeggio

The examples in this chapter apply the patterns we have developed thus far to the Major ii-V-I sequence. When two patterns are shown in brackets, the first pattern applies to the Dm7 chord and the second to the G7 chord.

Example 4b: [1-b7-b3-5] [1-b7-3-5]

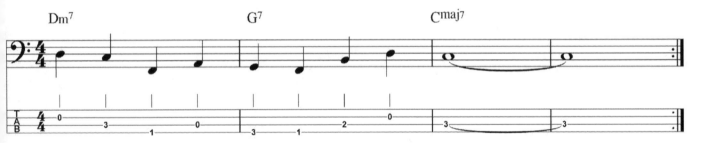

Example 4c: [1-b7-5-b3] [1-b7-5-3]

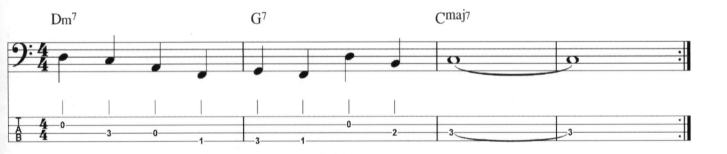

Example 4d: [1-1-b3-5] [1-5-8-5]

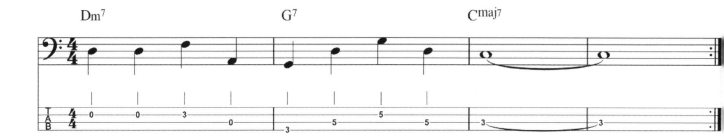

Example 4e: [1-5-b3-5] [1-8-b7-5]

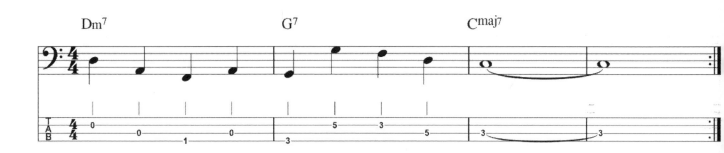

Example 4f: [1-1-5-b3] [1-3-5-3]

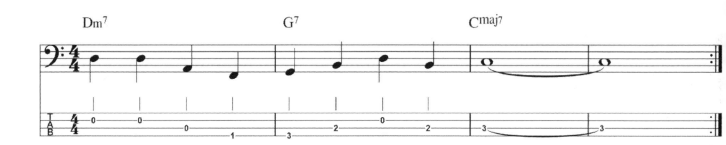

Example 4g: [1-b7-5-b3] [1-5-8-3]

Example 4h: [1-1-5-1] [1-3-5-3]

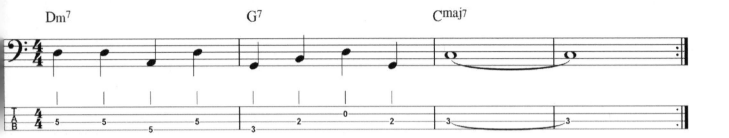

Example 4i: [1-b3-5-1] [8-b7-5-1]

In Example 4j, the same pattern applies to both the Dm7 and G7 since both chords have a flat 7th.

Example 4j: [1-b7-5-b5]

Example 4k: [1-b3-5-b5] [1-3-5-b5]

29

In Example 4l, we play both the Minor 3rd and Major 3rd of each chord for chromaticism. In the Dm7 chord, the Major 3rd is the non-chord tone, and in the G7 the Minor 3rd is the non-chord tone. The same concept applies to Examples 4m and 4n, with the Minor and Major 3rds, and the Perfect and flat 5ths (we'll discuss this more in Chapter Six).

Example 4l: [1-b7-b3-3]

Example 4m: [1-5-b3-3]

Example 4n: [1-2-5-b5]

Example 4o: [1-2-b3-5] [1-2-3-5]

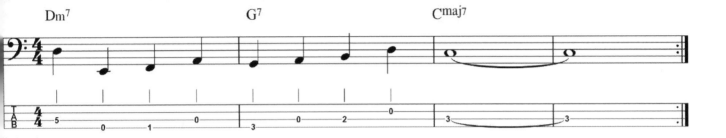

Example 4p: [1-2-6-5]

Example 4q: [1-b3-6-5] [1-3-6-5]

Example: 4r: [1-b7-6-5]

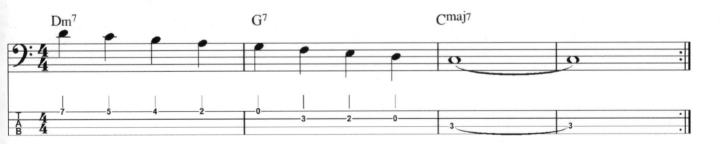

Example 4s: [1-1-2-b3] [1-1-2-3]

Example 4t: [1-2-b3-3]

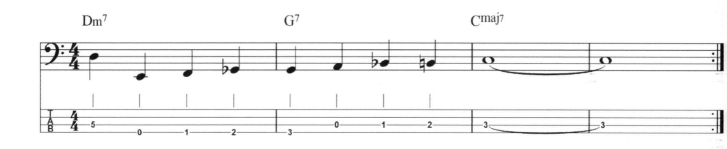

Chapter Five – The Jazz Blues Chord Progression

In this chapter, we will look at the "Jazz Blues" chord progression. Think of it as the offspring of the traditional blues and the Major ii-V-I.

The first seven bars are the same as the traditional blues, but in bar eight we move to an A7 chord to create a I-VI-ii-V progression. Notice that there is one chord per bar in bars seven to ten, and there are two chords per bar in bars eleven and twelve.

Jazz blues progression

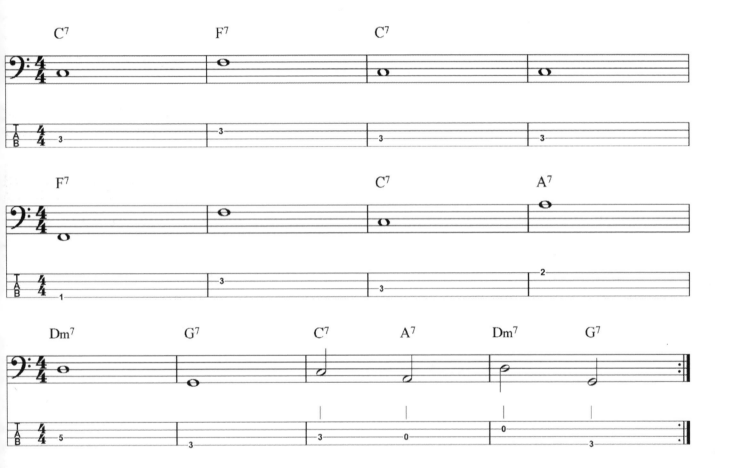

Moving from I to VI

We have built bassline patterns for all of the chord changes we'll need for the jazz blues with the exception of one, which is the movement from chord I to chord VI. When we harmonize the Major scale, the chord built off the 6th degree is a Minor seventh chord (m7). However, in the jazz blues this chord is typically played as a Dominant 7 (7).

Example 5a is a triad that approaches the root of the A7 chord chromatically from below.

Example 5a: [1-3-5-b6]

Example 5b walks chromatically down to the root of the A7 chord after hitting the root (C) twice.

Example 5b: [1-1-7-b7]

Example 5c revisits a common pattern we used for the I to IV movement, but it functions differently here. Instead of approaching the root of the A7 chord chromatically, it approaches from an E note, which is a perfect 5th away.

Example 5c: [1-2-b3-3]

Example 5d is our old friend the "change run" that we used when ascending from I to IV. Since it lands on the 5th (G) before the chord change, it works equally well here.

Example 5d: [1-2-3-5]

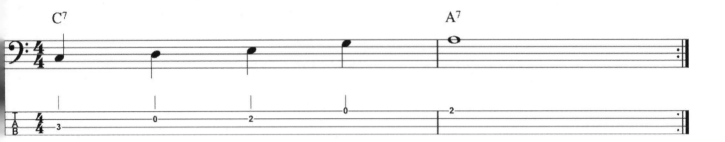

Example 5e is the ascending Dominant 7 arpeggio that we began with in Chapter Two, which approaches the root of the A7 chord (A) by a half step from above.

Example 5e: [1-3-5-b7]

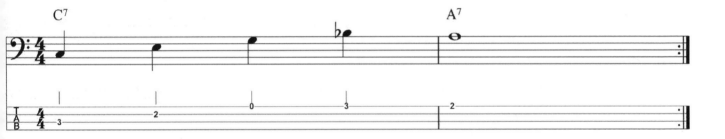

ii-V Setup

An interesting way to approach a chord change is to outline an "implied ii-V". This is often used over the last bar of a static chord to approach a new chord. In Example 5f, we are approaching the F7 chord, so think in terms of a ii-V-I with F as the I chord. This would be Gm7-C7-Fmaj7. These chords are not actually part of the tune, but we craft a bassline around them assuming they are!

Notice how nicely this approaches the root of the F7 chord.

Example 5f: [5-2-1-5]

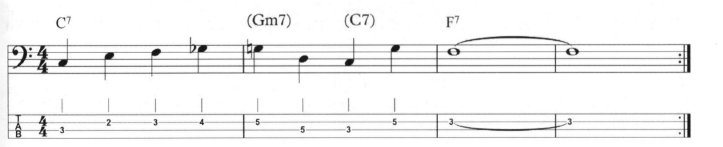

Two Chords per Bar

In the jazz blues, we often encounter songs with two chords in a bar instead of just one. Since each chord lasts only two beats, we only have two 1/4 notes to play over each chord. If we continue to play the root on beat one, we are left with just one available note to approach the next chord. In Examples 5g through 5i, the first pattern in brackets applies to bar one and the second to bar two.

Example 5g: [1-3] [1-b5]

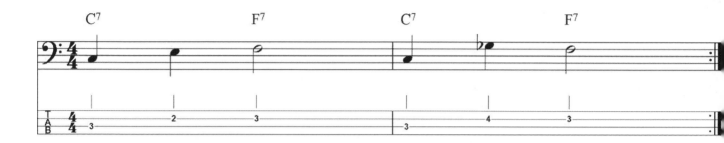

In Example 5h, the same pattern works equally well for both I to IV and I to VI movement.

Example 5h: [1-5]

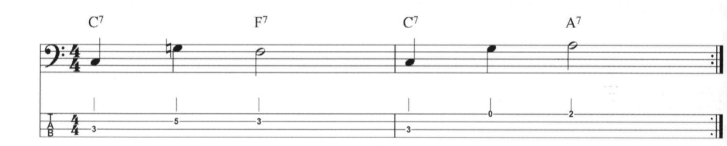

Example 5i: [1-2] [1-3]

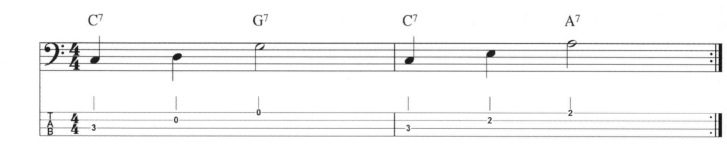

Table 5a: Summary of Bassline Patterns

I - VI	[1-3-5-b6] [1-1-7-b7] [1-2-b3-3]
	[1-2-3-5] [1-3-5-b7]
ii-V Setup (I-IV)	[5-2-1-5]
Two chords per bar I-IV	[1-3] [1-b5] [1-5]
Two chords per bar I-V	[1-2]
Two chords per bar I - VI	[1-5] [1-3]

Example 5j demonstrates a bassline over the jazz blues using the patterns that we have developed thus far. Play through this exactly as it is written, then experiment with some of the other patterns that you like.

Example 5j: Jazz Blues

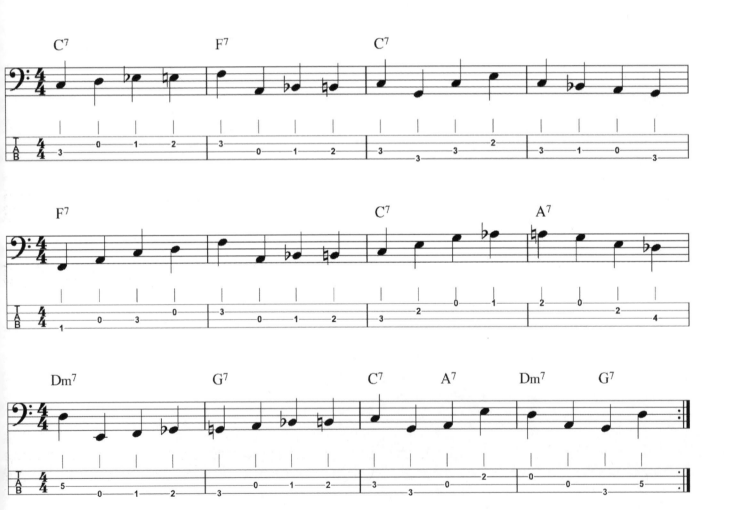

Chapter Six – The Minor ii-V-i

In Chapter Four, we developed walking basslines over the Major ii-V-I chord progression. In this chapter, we will develop basslines over the Minor ii-V-i chord progression, which consists of the chords built from the 1st, 2nd and 5th degrees of the Harmonic Minor scale.

When we harmonize this scale, the chord built off the root is a Minor/Major Seventh (mMaj7)(1-b3-5-7), the chord built off the 2nd degree is a Minor 7 Flat Five (m7b5)(1-b3-b5-b7), and the chord built off the 5th is a Dominant Seventh chord (7)(1-3-5-b7).

Example 6a shows a Minor ii-V-i in the key of Am, outlined with roots and 5ths. In this progression, the Bm7b5 to E7 is the ii to V movement and the E7 to Am is the V to I movement.

As with the Major ii-V-I, these chords also descend by a perfect 5th/ascend by a perfect 4th so we can apply similar patterns.

Chord ii is Bm7b5

Chord V is E7

Chord I is Am

Example 6a:

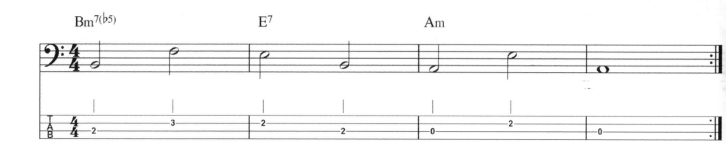

The ii chord in this progression is a m7b5 and, due to its flat 5th (b5), sounds much different than the m7 chord of the Major ii-V-I. It is important to emphasize this note in our basslines to bring out the unique flavor of this chord. The m7b5 chord arpeggio is shown below.

m7b5 Arpeggio

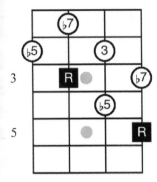

The tonic chord (AmMaj7) is quite dissonant and not normally suitable as a tonic, so it is normally substituted for a straight A minor. This is normally played as a simple Am triad, or an Am6 for a little extra colour.

The following examples demonstrate the I to IV patterns applied to the Minor ii-V-i. When two patterns are shown in brackets, the first pattern applies to the Bm7b5 chord and the second to the E7 chord.

Example 6b: [1-b7-3-b5] [1-b7-3-5]

Example 6c: [1-b7-b5-3] [1-b7-5-3]

Example 6d: [1-b5-3-b5] [1-5-3-5]

Example 6e: [1-1-b3-b5] [8-5-1-5]

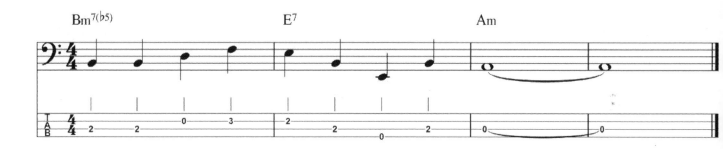

Example 6f: [8-b5-b3-b5] [1-8-b7-5]

Example 6g: [1-1-b5-b3] [1-3-5-3]

Example 6h: [8-7-b5-b3] [8-5-1-3]

Example 6i: [1-1-b5-1] [1-3-5-1]

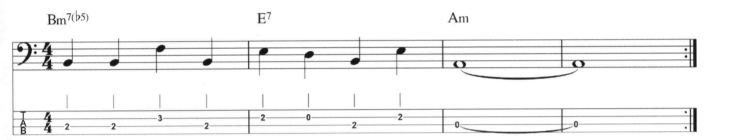

Example 6j: [1-b3-b5-8] [8-b7-5-1]

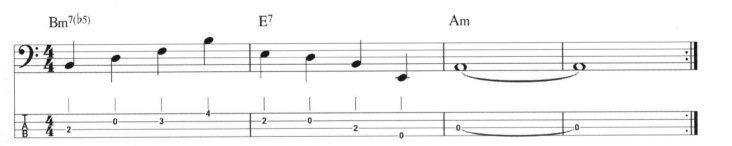

The patterns in Examples 6k through 6m don't outline the m7b5 chord particularly well because they include both the 5th and b5th, so we reserve them for the Dominant seventh (7) chord. We can play any other pattern we have developed thus far over the m7b5 chord.

Example 6k: [1-b3-b5-8] [1-b7-5-b5]

Example 6l: [8-b7-b5-1] [1-3-5-b5]

In Example 6m, we play the flat 2nds (b2) of Bm7b5 and E7 (C and F, respectively), rather than the natural 2nds (C# and F#). These b2s and natural 2s are somewhat interchangeable but playing the flat 2nds evokes the more exotic feel of the Harmonic Minor scale. We continue using the b2 through all of the following examples, but feel free to experiment with the sounds of the natural 2 also.

Example 6m: [1-b2-b3-b5] [1-b2-5-b5]

Example 6n: [1-b7-b3-3]

Example 6o: [1-b5-b3-3] [1-5-b3-3]

Example 6p: [1-b2-b3-3]

Example 6q: [1-b2-b3-b5] [1-b2-3-5]

Example 6r: [1-b2-6-b5] [1-b2-6-5]

Example 6s: [1-b3-6-b5] [1-3-6-5]

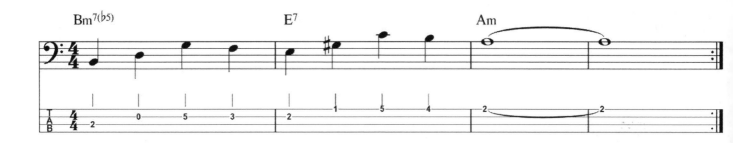

Example 6t: [1-b7-6-b5] [1-b7-6-5]

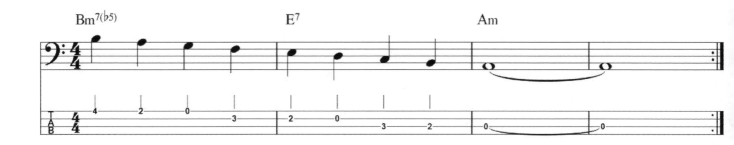

Example 6u: [1-1-b2-b3] [1-1-b2-3]

Example 6v shows a sequence similar to the A section of the famous jazz standard, Autumn Leaves. This is an important tune to have under your fingers because it consists of descending 5th movements, moving through both the Major and Minor ii-V-I chord progressions.

First, play through the bassline exactly as I have written it, then substitute the patterns above one at a time before combining them with some others you like to play.

Example 6v: Autumn Leaves Style Sequence

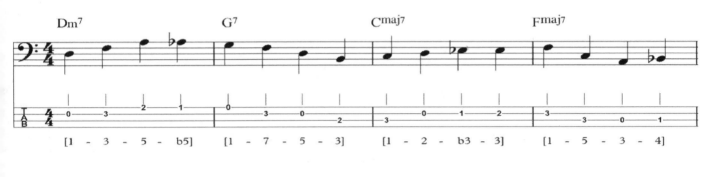

Chapter Seven – Other Common Chord Progressions

So far, we have looked at the following common jazz and blues chord changes:

- Static chord

- I to IV (a.k.a. ii to V, V to I)

- I to V

- I to VI

- V to IV

We will now look at some of the remaining chord progressions you are likely to encounter.

Moving from I to III

The movement from I to III7 is quite a common movement in many genres of music. It is demonstrated here in the key of C. Make sure work on this idea in different keys, such as G (GMaj7 to B7), and Bb (BbMaj7 to D7).

Example 7a: [1-1-2-b3]

Example 7b: [1-2-5-4]

Example 7c: [1-3-5-4]

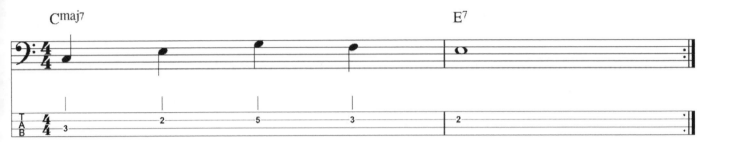

Example 7d: [1-7-1-2]

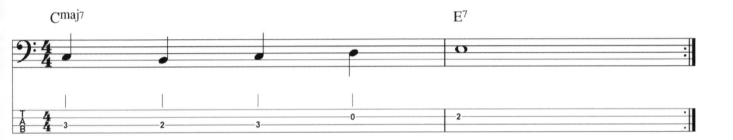

In Example 7e, the chromatic walk up creates a smooth chromatic walk from one root to the next!

Example 7e: [1-b2-2-b3]

Moving from Major to Minor

Sometimes the root of the chord doesn't change, but *quality* of the chord changes from Major to Minor. When this happens it's important to choose a pattern that highlights the 3rd (whether Major or Minor) of each chord to outline this change.

In Examples 7f and 7g, we use a static chord bassline over the D7 chord and can choose any pattern including a Minor 3rd over the Dm7 chord.

Example 7f: [1-3-1-5] [1-b3-5-b5]

Example 7g: [1-5-3-5] [1-2-b3-5]

Moving from I7 to II7

In Chapter Three we developed patterns moving a whole step down for a V7 to IV7 movement. Here we develop patterns moving a whole step up for I7 to II7 movement.

Example 7h: [1-5-3-b3]

Example 7i also functions as the chromatic walk up.

Example 7i: [1-b7-1-b2]

Example 7j: [1-5-4-3]

Example 7k: [1-3-5-6]

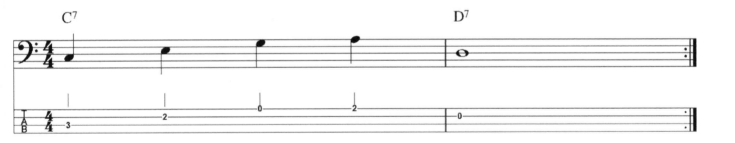

Example 7l: [1-5-1-3]

Example 7m shows the A section of another famous jazz standard, All of Me, that uses the I to III7 movement in the first two bars, Major to Minor shifts, and a lot of I to IV movement.

Example 7m: All of Me

Use this tune as a workhorse… substitute your own favorite patterns and experiment as much as you can. Find as many ways as possible to navigate the changes. Focus on approaching each chord change by a half step, whole step or a 5th.

Moving from i to bVI

While upper case Roman numerals denote Major chords, lower case numerals denote minor chords. In Examples 7n through 7q, the tonic chord is a C *minor* 6, and is therefore written as 'i', not 'I'.

The important thing to focus on is that we are moving from the root of some type of C chord to the root of some type of Ab chord, which is defined by i to bVI.

Example 7n: [1-2-b3-5]

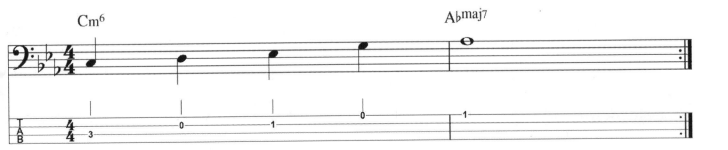

Example 7o walks chromatically down from the root of the Cm6 to the root of the AbMaj7.

Example 7o: [1-7-b7-6]

Example 7p ascends chromatically to the Minor 3rd (b3rd), which approaches the root of the Abmaj7 chord by a perfect 5th.

Example 7p: [1-b2-2-b3]

Example 7q is our old friend the "chromatic walk up" again, which we have shown can be used for any chord movement!

Example 7q: [1-4-b5-5]

Example 7r is the A section of the jazz standard, My Funny Valentine. It includes a static Cm chord with variations of the 7ths, i to bVI movement and a Minor ii-V-I progression.

Example 7r: My Funny Valentine

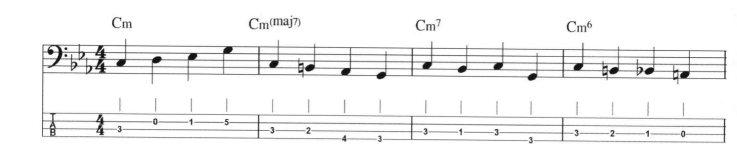

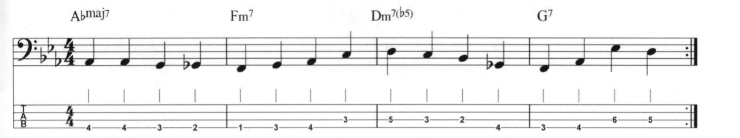

Table 7a: Summary of Bassline Patterns

I - III	[1-1-2-b3] [1-2-5-4] [1-3-5-4] [1-7-1-2] [1-b2-2-b3]
I - II	[1-5-3-b3] [1-b7-1-b2] [1-5-4-3] [1-3-5-6] [1-5-1-3]
i - bVI	[1-2-b3-5] [1-7-b7-6] [1-b2-2-b3] [1-4-b5-5]

Chapter Eight – Walking in 3/4 time

All the patterns we have developed so far are played in 4/4 time (four 1/4 notes per bar). When playing in 3/4 time, we have only three 1/4 notes to work with. We still play the root on beat one and an approach note on the final beat (beat three). We typically play a chord tone on beat two, but any note works if it sounds good.

In this chapter, we will develop patterns in 3/4 time for the common chord movement we have identified in previous chapters. We'll apply these patterns to m7, Maj7, Dom7 and m7b5 chords, so remember that when a pattern includes the 3rd, you play a Major 3rd over a Major chord and a Minor 3rd (b3rd) over a Minor chord. When the pattern includes a 7th, play a Major 7th over Maj7 chords and a Minor 7th over m7 and dom7 chords. When playing over a m7b5, you play a flat 5th.

Moving from I to IV (ii to V)

Example 8a is a Dm triad arpeggio that approaches the root of the G7 chord by a whole step from above. Triad arpeggios are great choices for I to IV movement because they outline the chord and always approach by a whole step.

Example 8a: [1-b3-5]

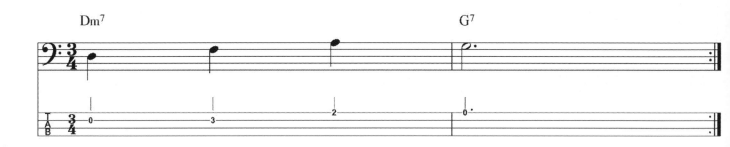

If you learn only one pattern for walking in 3/4 time, it should be the chromatic walk up. This smooth, chromatic pattern is easy to visualize and can be used repetitively over any chord progression.

Example 8b: [1-b3-3]

Think of Example 8c as a chromatic walk *down*.

Example 8c: [1-5-b5]

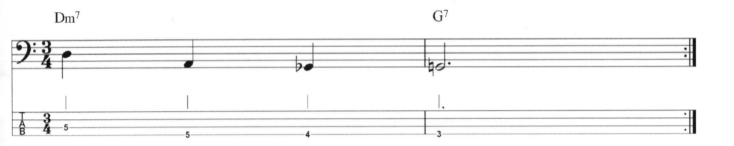

Example 8d walks up the scale to the root of the G7 chord.

Example 8d: [1-2-b3]

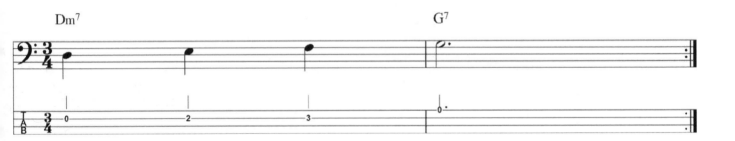

Example 8e is similar to Example 8a but moves to the melodic Major 6th note (B) on beat 2.

Example 8e: [1-6-5]

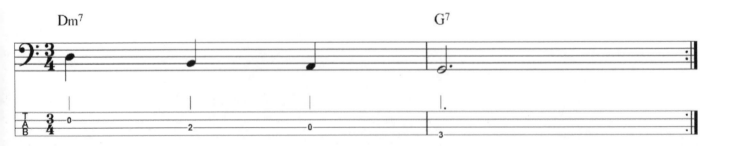

Examples 8f through 8h alternate between the root and the 3rd, 5th and 7th, and then approach the root of the G7 chord by a perfect 5th.

Example 8f: [1-b3-1]

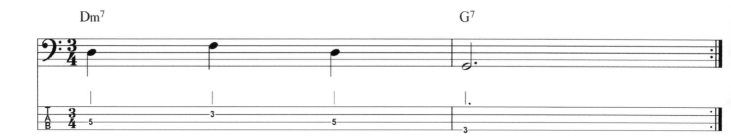

Example 8g: [1-5-1]

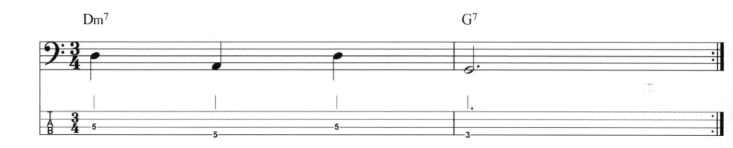

Example 8h: [1-b7-1]

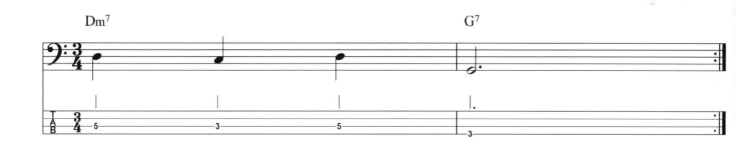

Moving from I to V

Example 8i: [1-6-b6] (chromatic walk down)

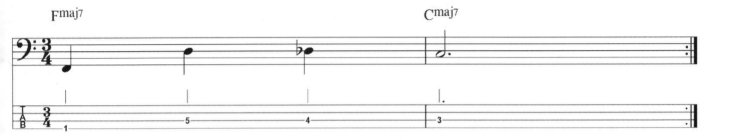

Example 8j: [1-4-b5] (chromatic walk up)

Example 8k walks down the scale to the root of the Cmaj7 chord.

Example 8k: [1-7-6]

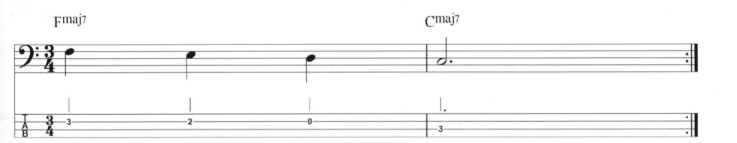

Example 8l approaches the root of the Cmaj7 chord from perfect 5th.

Example 8l: [1-b2-2]

Moving from i to ii

In Examples 8m to 8r we apply patterns for whole step movement to the i and ii chords of A Harmonic Minor.

Example 8m: [1-3-b3] (chromatic walk down)

Example 8n: [1-1-b2] (chromatic walk up)

Examples 8o through 8q alternate between the root and the 3rd, 5th and 7th to approach the root of the Bm7 chord by a whole step. These are the same patterns used in examples 8f through 8h for the I to IV movement, so you get twice the benefit by learning them!

Example 8o: [1-b3-1]

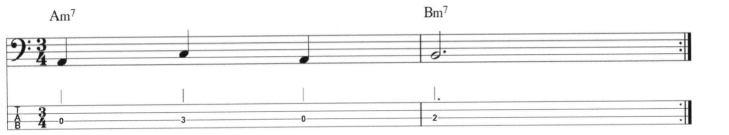

Example 8p: [1-5-1]

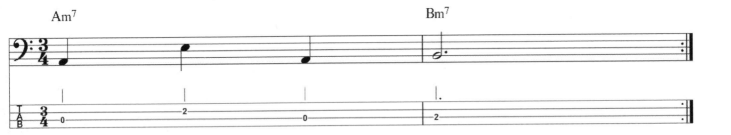

Example 8q: [1-b7-1]

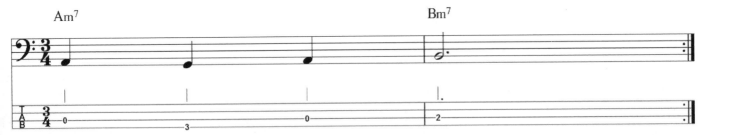

Example 8r is a triad arpeggio that approaches from above.

Example 8r: [1-5-b3]

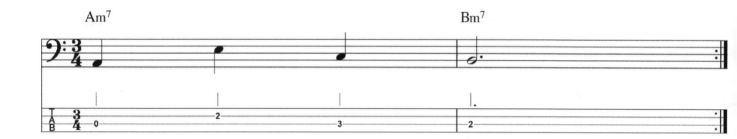

Moving from I to vi

Example 8s: [1-7-b7] (chromatic walk down)

Example 8t: [1-5-b6] (chromatic walk up)

Example 8u is a triad arpeggio that approaches from below.

Example 8u: [1-3-5]

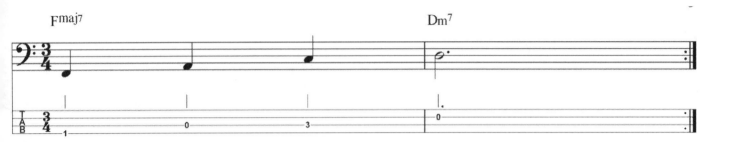

Example 8v hits the root twice, then walks down.

Example 8v: [1-1-7]

Example 8w walks up the scale and approaches the root of the Dm7 from a perfect 5th from below.

Example 8w: [1-2-3]

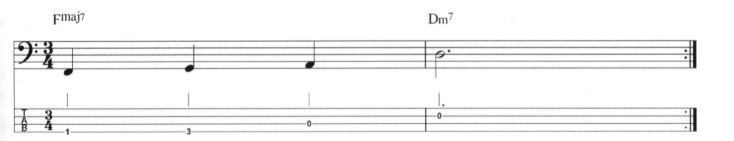

Static Chords

Example 8x: [1-b7-7] (chromatic walk up)

Example 8y is based on a common repeating blues bass riff, approaching from below.

Example 8y: [1-5-7]

Example 8z: [1-5-6]

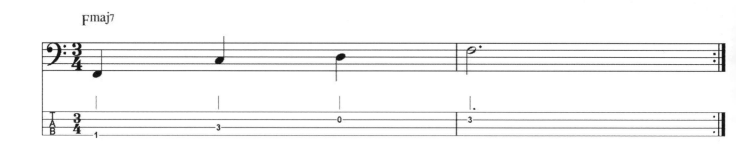

Examples 8z1 through 8z3 approach the root by a perfect 5th.

Example 8z1: [1-7-5]

Example 8z2 is based on a common Motown bass riff (think James Jamerson or Duck Dunn), also approaching from below.

Example 8z2: [1-6-5]

Example 8z3: [1-3-5]

Example 8z4 is the A section from the Rogers and Hammerstein classic, My Favorite Things. While most people know this as the song Julie Andrews taught the Von Trapp children to sing in The Sound of Music, it is also a jazz standard that has been covered by many famous musicians from Grant Green and John Coltrane to the Brian Setzer Orchestra.

Example 8z4: My Favorite Things

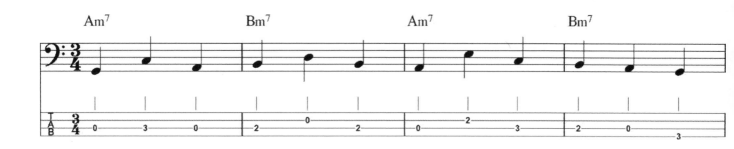

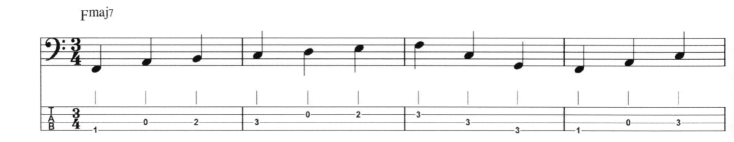

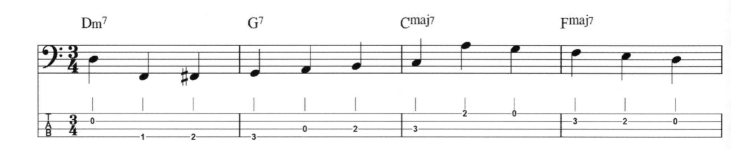

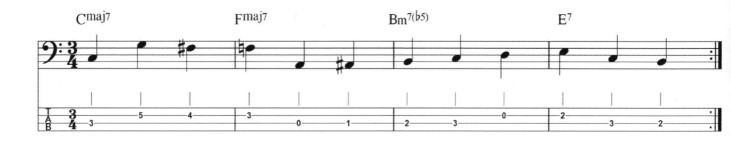

Table 8a: Summary of Bassline Patterns in 3/4

I to IV (ii to V)	[1-b3-5] [1-b3-3] [1-5-b5] [1-2-b3]
	[1-6-5] [1-b3-1] [1-5-1] [1-b7-1]
I to V	[1-6-b6] [1-4-b5] [1-7-6] [1-b2-2]
I to II (i to ii)	[1-3-b3] [1-1-b2] [1-b3-1] [1-5-1] [1-b7-1] [1-5-b3]
I to VI (I to vi)	[1-7-b7] [1-5-b6] [1-3-5] [1-1-7] [1-2-3]
Static Chord	[1-b7-7] [1-5-7] [1-5-6] [1-7-5] [1-6-5] [1-3-5]

Chapter Nine - Inversions

Nearly every pattern constructed so far has started with the root of the chord on beat one. While this is normally the most important note, it is possible to play other chord tones on beat one. When we play a chord tone other than the root, it is called an *inversion.*

Inversions are written down as the chord *over* the bass note. For example, a G7 chord with the note B in the bass would be written G7/B, and a G7 chord with the D in the bass would be written G7/D.

Using inversions on beat one can provide a melodic flow if used sporadically. However, the harmony of the chord is heard from the bass note up, so changing the root can change the way harmony is heard. For this reason, you should generally limit playing inversions to the most common chord movements (I to IV, I to V and static chords).

It's also a good idea to wait until you've played through the entire progression at least once before using an inversion so that the audience will become accustomed to hearing the harmony. For less common chord changes (I to III, I to VI etc.) it is best to play the root on beat one to emphasize the harmony as much as possible.

We'll revisit the Major ii-V-I progression in the key of C again.

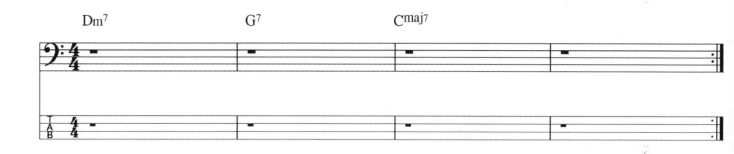

Let's use an inversion on the G7 chord.

The notes in a G7 chord are G, B, D and F. To create an inversion of this chord, we can play either a B, D or F on beat one of the bar.

When we play an inversion, the interval between the first note of the previous bar (Dm7) and the first beat of the G7 bar is changed. For example, without inversions we would play a bass pattern that moved from a bass note of D to a bass note of G. When we use an inversion on the G chord, we could be moving from the D on beat one of the previous Dm7 bar, to the notes B, D or F on beat one on the G7.

- If we play the note B on beat one of G7 *(1st inversion),* we can use any I to VI pattern over the Dm7 chord, since we are moving to the note B on the G7 chord. We move from Dm7 to G7/B.

- If we play the D on beat one of G7 *(2nd inversion),* we will play one of our static chord patterns because the note in the bass is static over the two bars. We move from Dm7 to G7/D.

- If we play an F on beat one of G7 *(3rd inversion),* we will play a I to bIII pattern.

But wait a minute, we haven't developed a I to bIII pattern! If you like the sound of this inversion, I encourage you to come up with a I to bIII pattern on your own. In reality, many of the I to III patterns will work with a little adjustment, but by now you are more than capable of creating walking bass patterns on your own.

Let's revisit the arpeggios we used to construct bassline patterns for the I to IV movement in Chapter One. In Example 9a, we rearrange the G7 arpeggio to play the 3rd (B) on beat one and play a I to VI pattern over the Dm7 chord. The patterns shown in brackets *apply to the inversion of the G7 chord.*

Example 9a: [3-1-b7-5]

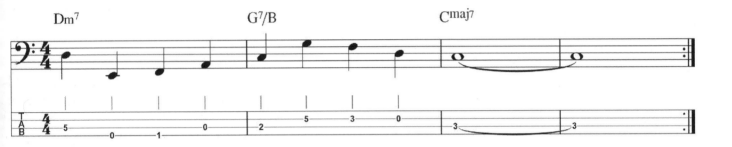

In Example 9b, we rearrange the G7 arpeggio to play the 5th (D) on beat one and play a static chord pattern over the Dm7 chord instead of a I to IV pattern.

Example 9b: [5-b7-1-3]

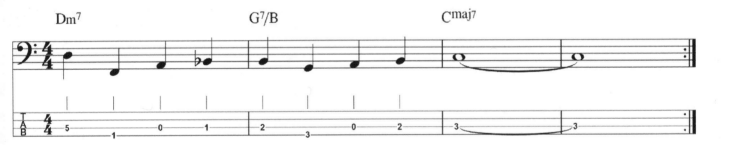

In Example 9c, we rearrange the G7 arpeggio to play the 7th (C) on beat one and play a I to bIII pattern over the Dm7. Since we haven't yet developed any I to bIII patterns, I'll give you a free one here!

Here we play a 1-b7-1-2 pattern over the Dm7 chord to approach the F of the G7 chord from below.

Example 9c: [b7-1-3-5]

In Examples 9a and 9c, the inversion on beat one is followed by the root note on beat two. This is generally good practice as it reinforces the tonality of the chord.

Regardless of whether we play a B, D or F on beat one of the G7 chord, we need to outline the rest of the G7 chord as we approach the Cmaj7 chord. In the previous examples we did this by playing a mixed-up arpeggio. However, we can include other scalar and chromatic notes too.

Since we play the root of the G7 chord on beat two most of the time, an easy way to approach the next chord is by playing the inversion on beat one (B, D or F), then playing a 3/4-time pattern starting with G to fill out the remaining three notes.

In Example 9d, we play a I to VI pattern to approach the B note on beat one of the G7 chord, then a three-note pattern starting on the G (beat two) of the G7 chord, approaching Cmaj7.

Example 9d: [3] [1-2-3]

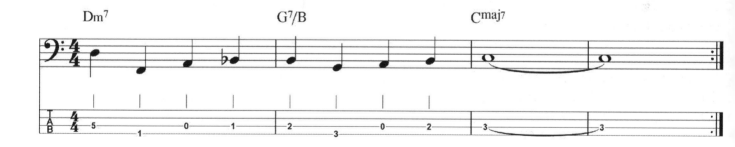

In Example 9e, we play a static chord pattern to approach the D note on beat one of the G7 chord, then a three-note pattern starting on G (beat two) of the G7 chord approaching Cmaj7.

Example 9e: [5] [1-3-5]

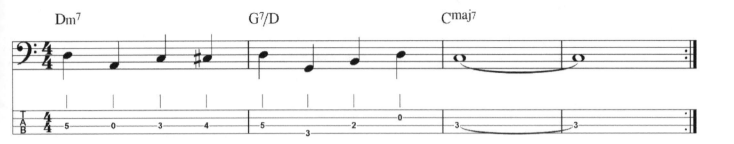

In Example 9f, we play a I to bIII pattern to approach the F note on beat one of the G7 chord, then a three-note pattern starting on G (beat two) of the G7 chord approaching Cmaj7.

Example 9f: [b7] [1-2-3]

In Example 9g, we revisit our old friend the Autumn Leaves progression, this time with inversions on every other chord. Inversions generally sound better in higher registers, but you can reinforce the tonality of the chord in lower registers by moving to the root on beat two, as we did in examples 9a through 9f.

While Example 9g is predominantly in the key of C, the G# of the E7 and the C# of the A7 chords are departures from the key, and therefore good to notes to emphasize. Even if you don't play them as inversions, you should include these notes in your bassline.

Example 9g: Autumn Leaves with Inversions

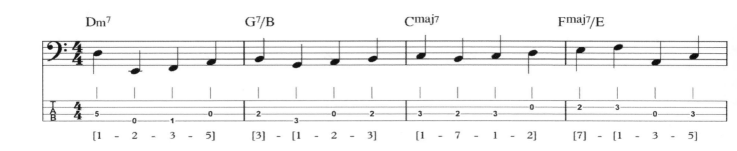

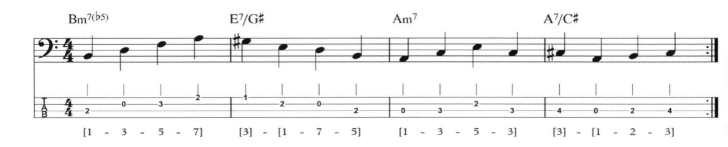

Static Movement

As we briefly discussed in Chapter Three, a common place to use inversions is over a static chord lasting more than one bar. The inversions are often played on the first beat of every second bar when the tonality of the chord is defined in bar one.

The most common note to use as an inversion is the 5th, but the 3rd and 7th are both valid too. Remember that we introduced this concept in Examples 3a and 3b, where we played the 7th and 5th respectively on beat one of bar two.

Example 3a: [1-3-5-6] [b7-6-5-3]

Example 3b: [1-3-4-b5] [5-4-3-2]

In Examples 9h through 9j, we play a I to V pattern in bar one to target the 5th of C (G) on beat one of bar two, followed by a I to IV pattern to return to the root on beat one of bar three. We have established that bass players generally think from the root up, and most of our patterns are created that way. By implying a G chord on beat one of bar two, we can play a pattern that starts on the root of a G chord rather than the 5th of a C chord.

Example 9h is a symmetrical pattern that goes up and back down to where it started over the course of two bars. The first pattern shown in brackets applies to the C7 chord and the second to the implied G.

Example 9h: [1-2-3-4] [1-b7-6-5]

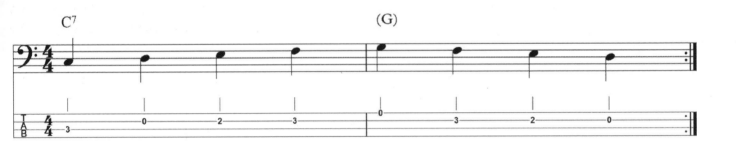

Example 9i ascends for two bars while Example 9j descends.

Example 9i: [1-3-4-b5] [1-2-b3-3]

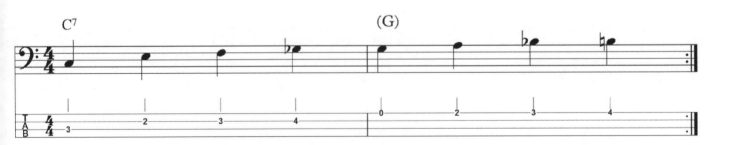

Example 9j: [1-b7-6-b6] [1-b7-6-5]

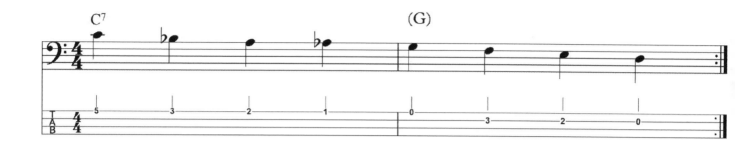

Example 9k demonstrates how you can combine Examples 9i and 9j to make an ascending and descending four-bar pattern, implying G chords on bars 2 and 4.

Example 9k:

Alternating between the root and the 5th on beat one of consecutive bars like this helps you to keep your place in songs that remain on one chord for multiple bars. Example 9l demonstrates a pattern over a sequence similar to the first eight bars of the Miles Davis classic, So What.

This song starts with sixteen bars of Dm7, followed by eight bars of Ebm7, ending with eight more bars of Dm7 and is notoriously difficult for keeping track of your location. By implying A chords on bars 2, 4, 6 and 8 and playing inversions, you can create longer two- and four-bar patterns that make it easier to keep track of where you are.

Example 9l: So What Style Progression

It is possible to create a smooth melodic line when playing over most chord changes that move in descending 5ths/ascending 4ths by moving from the 7th of one chord to the 3rd of the next. With this chord movement, the 3rds and 7ths of most chords are only a semitone apart, and at most a whole step. This technique of minimal movement between chord tones is called "voice leading".

In Example 9m, we play a C (b7th) on beat four of the Dm7 chord, followed by a B (3rd) on beat one of the G7 chord, which is a smooth half step interval. We extend the same idea to bars three and four, with a B (7th) on beat four of the Cmaj7 chord and an A (3rd) on beat one of the Fmaj7 chord.

Example 9m: Autumn Leaves Style with Voice Leading

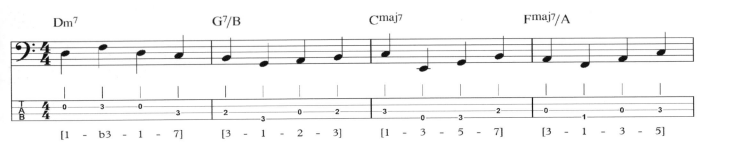

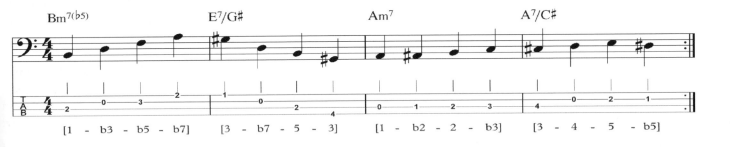

Chapter Ten - Rhythmic Variations

So far, we have focused on playing four 1/4 notes per bar. While this gives us a consistent walking bassline, we may want to sprinkle in some changes to the rhythmic pattern to allow the bassline to breathe a little better, giving it a little more of a human quality. Remember that our job as bassist is to keep time and lay down a predictable rhythm, so use these variations very sparingly.

We can mix up the rhythm by playing any note other than a 1/4 note, or even by inserting rests into the line. The point is to provide a brief departure from the consistency of the line, then return to it.

A common way to mix up the rhythm is to play two 1/8 notes in place of one 1/4 note. This can easily be done by playing the same note twice. In Example 10a, we play 1/8 notes on different beats throughout the first four bars of the blues progression. Try not to overthink this approach. Simply play two 1/8 notes in place of a 1/4 note sporadically throughout the progression when it feels right to you. If it feels forced, then it is not the right place!

Example 10a:

In Example 10b, we incorporate a variation on this idea by playing a muted or ghost note (indicated by an "x") for the second 1/8 note in each case. This percussive note gives the line a "hiccup" before moving on and sounds hipper than two normal 1/8 notes.

Example 10b:

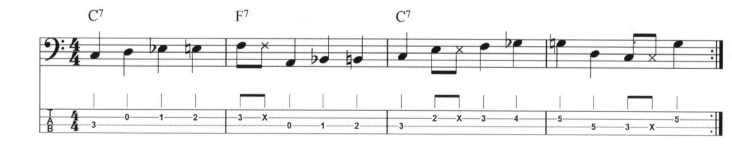

Similar to replacing a 1/4 note with two 1/8s, we can also play an 1/8 note triplet. It is best to reserve this for slower tempos until you have really gotten comfortable with it, since it is easy to lose the rhythm when playing at faster tempos. This is a common complaint of bassists among drummers.

Chromatic notes lend themselves well to triplets, since they can be played in succession quickly. In Example 10c, we insert a triplet by substituting a note in our pattern with a chromatic walk up (or walk down) to the next note in the pattern.

Example 10c:

In Example 10d we play the same note three times, which sounds best if we mute two of them.

Example 10d:

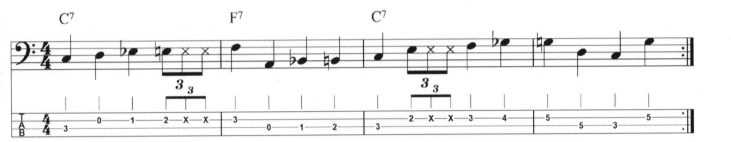

We can also use 1/4 note triplets to change up the rhythm. This time we will replace two 1/4 notes with a triplet instead of one as we did with 1/8 note triplets. This has an entirely different feel. Whereas the 1/8 note triplets feel like a burst of notes pushing the bassline forward, the 1/4 note triplets feel like they are briefly holding the bassline back. Example 10e demonstrates the feel of the 1/4 note triplet.

Example 10e:

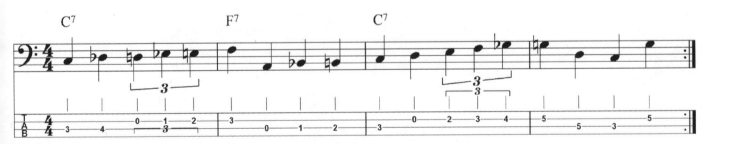

As we know, playing 1/4 notes is known as playing with a *four* feel. In Chapter One, we looked at playing half notes, which is known as playing with a *two* feel. While playing in four feels like *walking*, playing in two feels more like *dancing*. In Example 10f, we mix in some half notes to throw a little dance into our walk.

Example 10f:

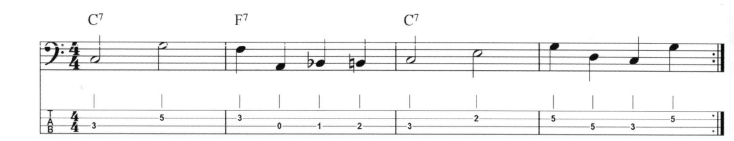

In Example 10g we add just enough rhythmic variation to the jazz blues to make it interesting without overdoing it.

Example 10g:

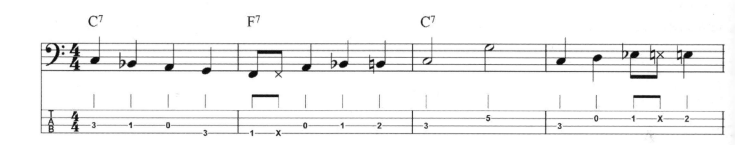

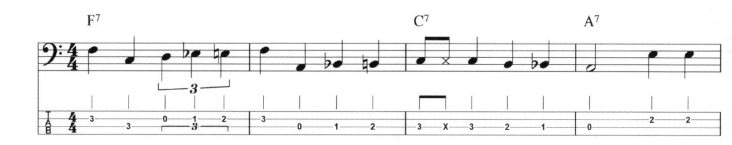

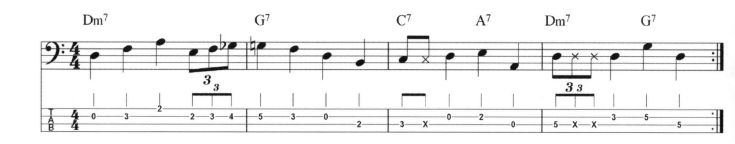

Putting It All Together

We have covered many bassline patterns for a variety of different chord progressions. There are certainly many more patterns that can be developed, but I have tried to stick to the ones that sound the best. We took an in-depth approach to developing these patterns, without getting too bogged down in theory. In almost all of these patterns, we simply connect the root notes of each chord with a series of scale and chord tones.

A good walking bassline must be consistent, played with notes of equal duration, volume and feel, to outline the chord progression and to reinforce the rhythm. If you are consistent most of the time, then any variations (rhythmic or note selection) you add as the song develops will sound fresh. It's important not to overdo these variations since you may lose the audience and the other musicians. A great bassline can stand alone: All of the other musicians could stop playing, but the harmony and the rhythm would still be heard through the bassline.

The most important thing you can do when playing any type of music is to memorize the chord progression. It's hard to create interesting and fluid lines while trying to figure out where you are in the song or what the next chord is. When learning a new song, write out the bassline pattern over each of the chords on the lead sheet.

Don't feel like you have to immediately memorise every pattern in this book. It's far better to write out a well-constructed bassline and learn to play it, than to make something up as you go (at least when you're starting out). Soon you will get these patterns under your fingers and the sounds in your head, and it will come much more naturally.

If you do find yourself lost during a song (which can sometimes happen to the best of us... especially during instrumental solos), remember that rhythm is most important consideration, and continue to thump out 1/4 notes, regardless of what they are. Most people won't even notice a few outside notes, but EVERYONE will notice if you break your rhythm or, worse, stop playing until you find your place. If you have laid down a consistent bassline up to the point of your mistake, people will just assume you meant to do it, and you are just exercising creative license!

I recommend developing "scripted basslines" for a few common progressions. For example, construct a bassline for the jazz blues progression that we developed in Chapter Five in the key of C. Once you have internalized this twelve bar pattern and are comfortable playing it, use it as the building block for new patterns, or fall back on it and play it note for note if necessary. Then take the bassline and play it in the keys of A and Bb. You will find that some patterns don't fit under your fingers quite as well as when playing in other keys, so adjust as necessary. If you memorize basslines in keys of A, Bb and C, then you can easily transfer them to the keys of E, F and G just by moving everything down a string. That's twice the value for your investment!

After you have learned your basslines for the jazz blues in three keys (trust me, it really won't take that long), move on to Autumn Leaves in G and Bb. This will force you to commit to memory basslines for Major and Minor ii-V-I's, which we have established as the most common chord progressions in jazz.

So, there you have it. If you've stuck with me through all of this, you should now be confident constructing a walking bassline that outlines any chord and smoothly approaches the next for any chord progression you encounter. Remember, playing music is about being creative and having fun. The more effort you put in, the more rewarding it will be.

On that note (pun intended), I'll leave you with a complete bassline for the George Gershwin classic, Summertime, using bits and pieces of everything we have developed in this book, including fragments of the melody. While we didn't discuss melody, suffice to say that learning the melody of a song and sprinkling bits of it in occasionally will make your bassline all the more melodic.

Dissect this bassline and figure out all of the patterns, inversions, ~~n~~ ~~ents,~~ then make it your own. But most importantly, be musical and hav~~e~~

Summertime Style Sequence

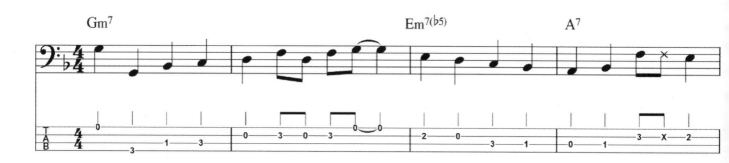

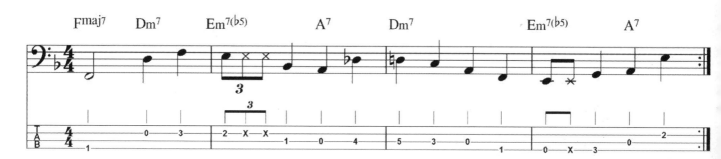